Original title:
Moonwalk Musings

Copyright © 2025 Creative Arts Management OÜ
All rights reserved.

Author: Cameron Blair
ISBN HARDBACK: 978-1-80567-811-3
ISBN PAPERBACK: 978-1-80567-932-5

Lunar Whispers

Under the glow, my shadow prances,
Trying to catch its own funny glances.
The moon winks with a silvery grin,
As I trip over thoughts of where I've been.

Crickets laugh at my silly ballroom,
While stars giggle in the cosmic room.
I dance with the breeze, wear socks on my feet,
In a wobbly rhythm, my two left feet.

Strolling through Starlight

On a cosmic path with twinkling sights,
I chase fireflies and silly flights.
The bunnies stretch their legs so wide,
While I fumble through this evening ride.

Puppies bark at comets that zoom,
As I step, I hear laughter in the gloom.
My hat flies away, oh what a sight,
Chasing it down feels just so light!

Echoes of the Night Sky

Echoes of laughter loop through the air,
As I try to dance like I haven't a care.
The stars are my audience, all aglow,
Cheering me on in this wondrous show.

I trip on my thoughts as they bounce around,
Each giggle and hiccup is a playful sound.
The night swells with joy, in a whimsical hug,
While the moon croons softly, just like a bug.

Reflections on a Silver Path

Wandering silver paths in the night,
I stumble on shadows that wiggle in fright.
The reflections chuckle, with glee they sway,
As I giggle back at my clumsy ballet.

Each step feels like riding a bouncy ball,
Gravity teasing, oh how we sprawl!
I grin at the swirl of this cosmic charade,
In a quirky waltz that won't ever fade.

Chasing the Moonlit Dream

Under a sky of silver beams,
I chased a frog named Jim,
He hopped and laughed a bright old laugh,
Said, "Catch me now, if you can swim!"

Around the park we made our flight,
With stars above and shadows tight,
We leaped on grass, so fresh, so green,
And left behind footprints of sheer delight.

Silhouettes in Ethereal Light

In ghostly shades we danced and spun,
Two shapes entwined, it was such fun,
A cat burst out, with half a meow,
Thought it was time for a midnight run!

We twirled in circles, hearts aglow,
Bumping our noses, oh what a show!
The crickets chirped a symphony,
As we found joy in the simple, slow.

Meditations at Midnight's Edge

Sat on a bench, my friend and I,
Contemplating how cheese could fly,
We laughed so hard we scared a deer,
Who pondered life with a doubtful eye.

With moonlight glowing, ideas soared,
We wrote our thoughts on a cardboard board,
A recipe for laughter, sprinkled with cheer,
A pinch of whimsy, and never bored!

The Dance of Celestial Bodies

The stars threw a party, a cosmic event,
We joined the dance, a little bent,
I tripped on air and landed like toast,
The universe giggled, it seemed so content.

We spun through meteors, a glittery shower,
With each little tumble, we gained our power,
At the end of it all, with a twinkle and grin,
We declared ourselves the rulers of hour!

Nocturnal Inspirations

The stars are winking, full of cheer,
A cat in pajamas, oh dear, oh dear!
A raccoon sneaking snacks, what a sight,
As I ponder the mysteries of the night.

The owls are hooting a comic tune,
While fireflies bust a move like a cartoon,
A dance with shadows beneath the trees,
As I giggle at the antics of the breeze.

Nighttime Contemplations

The snoring moon slips from its bed,
As crickets play chess in my head,
Tadpoles sing opera, off-key and loud,
While I chuckle away with the frogs in the crowd.

The stars throw a party, it's all so bright,
As squirrels debate the meaning of night,
With chocolate chip cookies up for a vote,
The funniest scene that I ever wrote.

Through the Veil of Night

A glowing lightbulb buzzes awake,
It must be the moon with a silly mistake,
An echo of laughter runs through the trees,
As shadows dance whimsically, oh please!

The night sky giggles, tickling my feet,
With comets playing tag, how sweet!
I can't help but laugh, my head in the clouds,
As I join in the fun, giggling proud.

Silvery Reflections

The lake is a mirror, all glimmer and shine,
With ducks quacking jokes, oh how divine!
A fish leaps up, wearing a grin,
While the moon snickers softly, ready to spin.

The trees whisper secrets, they can't keep,
As sleep bugs tap dance, not a soul to weep,
I laugh at the wise old owl's silly hat,
As the night flirts with dreams—it's a humorous spat.

Light Amongst Shadows

In the dark where giggles hide,
A flashlight beams, laughter's guide.
Shadows dance upon the ground,
Chasing echoes, joy's sweet sound.

Footsteps slip, a silly trip,
Bouncing off the walls with a quip.
Whispers tease the night away,
As shadows laugh, they join the play.

Hiding here with a playful glance,
Under stairs, we sneak and prance.
With every flicker, fun ignites,
In the shadows, laughter lights.

Echoing tales of nighttime cheer,
Every giggle, fun draws near.
In this dance, we find our bliss,
A shadow's secret, a giggle's kiss.

Skyline Serenade

Stars on rooftops twinkle bright,
City tales under moonlight.
Singing soft, the skyline hums,
As clumsy pigeons dance and strum.

A cat leaps high, it misses the height,
Crash landing, what a funny sight!
The skyline laughs with every fall,
As city whispers echo the call.

With a slingshot, dreams take flight,
Flying cars zoom past the night.
Giant balloons float overhead,
In this serenade, laughter's fed.

Beneath the lights, we twirl and spin,
Chasing whims, let the fun begin!
In this urban jest, we sing,
A humorous dance, city's fling.

A Dance with the Cosmos

Starry nights invite a jig,
Cosmic friends join, feeling big.
Asteroids bounce, they whirl and sway,
In this choreography of play.

Gravity's prank makes us float,
Laughter bubbles in each quote.
With every twist, a comet slips,
Wobbling, giggling, cosmic trips.

Planets spin, a merry waltz,
With every whirlwind, no one faults.
Galaxies tease with a wink,
Dance with stars, forget to think.

In the universe's sly embrace,
We find joy in this wild chase.
A dance with laughter fills the air,
Cosmic musings, a jolly affair.

Ethereal Ramblings

Floating high on fluff and dreams,
Clouds whisper silly, bright moonbeams.
Chasing rainbows, we skip along,
In this whimsy, we belong.

Bubbles burst with giggles strange,
Funny faces, what a range!
The air is light with jesting puns,
As starlight twirls and brightly runs.

With every step, we lose our way,
In this realm where jesters play.
Gravity begs us not to land,
But we dance with dreams, hand in hand.

Echoes of laughter fill the night,
In this celestial frolic, pure delight.
Ethereal spirits laugh and glide,
In our ramblings, joy won't hide.

Galaxies in Motion

In a rocket made of cheese,
I zoom past stars with ease.
The Martians wave and laugh out loud,
My spaceship's just a screwy cloud.

Asteroids tumble, roll, and bounce,
I dodge them like a clumsy flounce.
Neptune's got a gloomy frown,
But I just spin my head around.

Twilight Thoughts

Under skies that twinkle bright,
  I ponder if I'll fly tonight.
A comet tail made out of beans,
  I'm the king of silly dreams.

Constellations dance and sway,
  Orion's lost his pants today!
  I giggle as I float and glide,
Through this cosmic, starry slide.

Echoes of the Celestial

Singing stars with funny tunes,
They bop and weave like silly loons.
Jupiter's got a playful grin,
While Saturn sports a hula hoop spin.

Galaxies swirl in a jolly jig,
I try to join, but trip, oh big!
A nebula's a swirling dress,
I'm amazed by all this mess!

Silhouettes in Silver

Luna's cast a shadow game,
And stars are playing all the same.
With cosmic giggles high above,
They tease me like a playful dove.

I tiptoe on a moonbeam bright,
But oh! I slipped, what a sight!
The sun's just laughing, bright and bold,
While I stumble in space, uncontrolled.

Interstellar Dreams in Silhouette

In space, my sandwich flies,
A comet made of cheese and fries.
With astronauts who laugh and tease,
I float along with cosmic ease.

The stars are shaped like silly hats,
And dancing cows, oh, how they prance!
Galaxies hum a tune so sweet,
While I twirl in my moonlit feat.

A telescope, my trusty mate,
Brings distant worlds and laughter great.
With every glance, the fun unfolds,
In this wild realm, where joy beholds.

So here I drift, with dreams of cheer,
Among the stars, I hold so dear.
In this vast playground, I delight,
Where cosmic giggles take their flight.

Wanderings Beneath a Velvet Sky

Beneath the deep, the sky unzips,
A blanket where the starlight slips.
With every twinkle, laughter grows,
As fireflies join the cosmic shows.

A meteor like popcorn bursts,
In sky-blue butter, joy immersed.
With moonbeams soft as cotton candy,
We share our dreams, quite sweet and dandy.

The planets dance in silly spins,
Creating mischief, grins and grins.
A cosmic car, we take a ride,
With laughter echoing far and wide.

At last we pause, just you and me,
In this starlit, wild jubilee.
With goofy grins and sparkly eyes,
We drift beneath these velvet skies.

Lunar Reverie

Oh, what a laugh on lunar shores,
Where ants hold parties with no chores.
With each jump, they reach for the light,
In this round world of sheer delight.

A bunny floats, adorned in bows,
With carrot cake, the party grows.
We toast with flares, and giggles newly,
In this odd world, we dance so freely.

The moon is just a giant cheese,
And all my friends come here to tease.
In this wacky dream, we build our throne,
Made of star-dust and giggles grown.

With every bounce, our worries flee,
In this wild land of pure jubilee.
So here's to laughter, bold and bright,
In a lunar dream, oh, what a night!

Starlit Soliloquy

In a galaxy of minty lights,
Where ants wear ties and take to flights.
They sip on slushies made of dreams,
While cosmic jellybeans split at seams.

A comet spins a yarn so wild,
Of space-bound cats, each one a child.
They frolic in this stardust stew,
With jokes that sparkle, fresh and new.

I chat with planets, oh such fun,
As they play games of peek-a-boo run.
With giggles echoing, loud and clear,
In this bewitching cosmic sphere.

So here I sit, on this bright cloud,
With interstellar jesters, loud.
In every twinkle, laughter beams,
In a universe of joyful dreams.

Phases of Reflection

In the sky, I see it glow,
The cheese-shaped orb puts on a show.
I tried to take a selfie there,
But I just caught my messy hair.

It winked at me, its silver beam,
As if to say, 'It's all a dream!'
I danced beneath its gentle light,
And tripped on toes—it felt just right.

Starry-Eyed Longing

Gazing up, I see a friend,
A bright ball that won't pretend.
It whispers secrets from afar,
I think it's flirting, what a star!

I wish I had a cosmic ride,
To orbit it with silly pride.
But here I am, just standing still,
Mixing punch with moonlit chill.

Walking with the Cosmos

I took a step, then slipped and fell,
As stardust giggled; can you tell?
The path was paved with lunar dust,
And I just knew I'd trip; I must!

As I frolicked with starry friends,
Conversations had no real ends.
I claimed the moon; it stayed aloof,
And laughed as I just lost my proof.

Midnight Chronicles

At midnight, when the world's asleep,
I chat with shadows, secrets keep.
The crickets chirp, a cosmic tune,
While I debate with forks and spoons!

The stories shared beneath the sky,
Of silly waves that made me cry.
The universe, my quirky mate,
Keeps laughing at our silly fate.

Chronicles of the Night

In the dark, I trip and fall,
My shadow dances on the wall.
A soft breeze teases my hair,
I laugh at the moon's playful stare.

Starlit whispers in my ear,
Are those giggles? Oh dear, oh dear!
Raccoons join in, a crazy crew,
They think it's fun—what about you?

The owl hoots, quite a scholar,
I turn to him—give me the dollar!
My wallet's lost, it's quite a fight,
I guess I'll dance with the moon tonight!

Chasing thoughts in the night's embrace,
Tripping over in this crazy race.
The cosmos chuckles, what a sight,
Laughing with me till morning light!

Cosmic Contemplations

Stars twinkle like they're in a show,
I wonder if they have a glow-to-flow.
Dodging meteors with a silly grin,
Can't they see? I've got to win!

Planets spin in a dizzy blur,
I'm a space dancer, that's for sure!
With a leap and a wink, I float so high,
Trying to catch a comet's eye.

Rocket ships zoom by with flair,
But I'm on foot, searching for air.
Galactic jokes fill the void so wide,
In this cosmic circus, I take pride!

Wormholes bend, oh what a twist,
Falling through is not on my list.
Yet here I am, making a scene,
Cracking jokes with Neptune's queen!

Dances of the Dark

Moonlit jig on a midnight stage,
I'm the star in this cosmic cage.
Down I twirl, hopping with glee,
Who knew darkness could dance with me?

The night is young, let's hit the floor,
Bumping into crickets—what's in store?
A funky beat from a firefly band,
I kick my feet in the soft, cool sand.

Whispers float like confetti in air,
The stars clink glasses, a celestial fair.
As I juggle with joy, I trip once more,
The universe laughs, I can't hit the floor!

Dancing clumsily under the sky,
Evading clouds that just pass by.
In the theater of night, I find my spark,
Leaving my mark in this dance of dark!

Celestial Conversations

Talking to stars across the abyss,
I'm convinced they share my bliss.
Jupiter chuckles, Saturn rolls eyes,
Conspiracies fly, and laughter flies.

Whiffs of stardust, tales unfold,
Silly antics from the starry old.
Venus claims she can outshine,
But I'm still here, sipping moonshine!

Galaxies gossip, trading their best,
Who's got the shiniest cosmic vest?
I join in with jokes from Earth's view,
Mortals laugh—what a funny crew!

While comets sweep by like giggling kids,
The universe winks, never quite hid.
In the tapestry of night's vibe,
We're all part of a cosmic tribe!

Wonder Under the Stars

Under the night sky, I trip and fall,
Stars laugh above, like they've seen it all.
I dance with shadows, what a silly sight,
The cosmos snickers, in the pale moonlight.

A comet zooms by, it winks at me,
"Can you keep up?" Oh, the cosmic glee!
I stumble and giggle, my shoes untied,
As the universe chuckles, I let joy glide.

The planets are swirling, what a wild crowd,
They cheer me on, oh, how I'm avowed!
I moonwalk my way to a starry game,
Jupiter spins while I shout its name.

In this silly ballet, I'm the star tonight,
The void around sparkles, with pure delight.
So here's to the cosmos, let laughter abide,
For under the stars, I'm along for the ride.

Cosmic Traces

I left my mark on a shooting star,
A little bit of sparkle, from way afar.
My footprints in space, a wobbly trace,
As aliens chuckle, I'm lost in the race.

Gliding through galaxies, I twist and shout,
In zero gravity, there's no doubt!
With a giggle or two, I float like a kite,
Past meteors dancing, into the night.

I wave to the planets, they're throwing a rave,
Uranus just giggled; oh, what a wave!
From one end of the cosmos to the other with flair,
Life's a big joke when you float through the air.

So let's chase the stars, to laughter we cling,
With every little hop, let the universe sing.
Round and round in this cosmic embrace,
Funny how I find joy in this vast, silly space.

Fragments of Night

Gather 'round, moonbeams, let's share a laugh,
I'll tell you a tale, from the starlit path.
With each silly twirl, I spin on a beam,
The night's full of chuckles, oh what a dream!

Meteors whisper, "You dance like a fool!"
While Saturn just spins by, breaking the rule.
I slip on a star, tumble into the void,
In this chaos of giggles, I'm happily buoyed.

The craters on the moon listen to my song,
They chuckle and nod, singing along.
A cosmic conga line? I've started a craze,
Let's laugh through the cosmos in whimsical ways!

In fragments of night, each star plays a part,
With a wink and a nudge, they all warm my heart.
So let's swirl through the dark, hold on tight to our cheer
For a universe filled with laughter is what we hold dear.

Celestial Guidance

Oh, starlit counsel, what wisdom you lend,
With comets and quips, the night we transcend.
I ask the bright moon for funny advice,
"Just trip and keep dancing, it'll all suffice!"

With a chuckle from Venus, the joke takes flight,
"Fumble your steps and you'll shine oh so bright!"
Mars adds a snicker, a wink in its glare,
"Who knew funky moves could dance with such flair?"

Galaxies giggle, unyielding in grace,
As I twirl and I spin, find joy in the chase.
Jupiter's laughter fills the void of space,
Offering chuckles in this star-studded race.

So here's to the sky and its luminous jest,
Each laugh from a star, an unwavering quest.
In celestial guidance, where humor is found,
We twirl in the night, forever spellbound.

Tread Lightly Under Stars

Underneath the twinkling lights,
I stumbled on my shoelace twice.
With every step, the crickets sang,
I tripped and danced, oh what a prance!

The moon grinned down upon my woes,
As I struck poses, striking blows.
I laughed so hard, I lost my breath,
In this waltz of cosmic jest, no death.

The constellations wink with glee,
As I pirouette, oh look at me!
A stardust trail I leave behind,
In this clumsy ballet, I'm so refined.

So if you wander through the night,
Beware of knees and sudden flight.
For in the space of stars and dreams,
I bring mishaps, or so it seems!

Cosmic Echoes

Floating past a comet's tail,
I tried to surf; it ended in fail.
I winked at Jupiter, filled with cheer,
And accidentally called him 'Dear'.

The rings of Saturn sang my song,
But I forgot the lyrics—how wrong!
I jived with asteroids, dancing bold,
Who knew space rocks could be so cold?

In cosmic realms, my belly aches,
From laughing hard at silly mistakes.
With Martian friends, I shared a snack,
And tossed my chips to a wayward quack.

Around the stars, I made my rounds,
In zero G, I tumbled—oh, sounds!
Echoing giggles through the night,
Who knew space could feel so bright?

Celestial Journey

A rocket ride to realms unknown,
Where laughter's fuel is brightly shone.
I packed some snacks, a comic book,
Who knew the stars would get me hooked?

Through galactic trails, I zipped and zoomed,
In this vast dance, I felt consumed.
I waved at aliens, said 'What's up?'
They offered me a glowing cup!

With stardust ice cream, cosmic treats,
I tripped on clouds beneath my feet.
A nebula formed a playful swirl,
And in that chaos, I did twirl.

So join me on this starry spree,
With giggles shared and joy to see.
For every bump and every laugh,
In space, we find our silly path!

Reflections in the Dark

In shadows cast by lunar rays,
I found my way in funny ways.
Each step a slip, each breath a grin,
The universe laughed, I joined in!

With silly hats from cosmic sales,
And echoes of my past fails,
I saw my face in starry ink,
Could galaxies blush? Oh, let me think!

A mirror ball of nebulae bright,
Reflected all my blunders right.
I juggled moons with wobbly glee,
A cosmic clown, just let me be!

So if you peek in night's embrace,
You might just find my wobbly grace.
For every stumble in the dark,
Turns into laughter—what a spark!

Beneath the Celestial Glow

Underneath the shining orb,
I tripped on my own two feet.
The stars laughed, a celestial mob,
As I danced to an offbeat.

The crickets chirped their tune,
While I lost my sense of grace.
I spun 'round like a cartoon,
With bug bites all over the place.

A raccoon joined my jig,
Wearing my snack on its nose.
We twirled in the moonlight gig,
Stepping on toes, who knows?

Laughter echoed through the night,
As I stumbled on grass so wet.
In the glow, laughter took flight,
And I swear I won't forget.

Glimmers of a Soft Dream

In the night, my thoughts take flight,
With visions as silly as can be.
Unicorns dance in their delight,
Wearing socks and sipping tea.

I chased a cloud on a bright kite,
It swirled and dodged with glee.
It led me to a funky sight,
A fish that sang like a bee.

Caught in giggles, I spun around,
As owls hooted in surprise.
The moon kept grinning, quite profound,
While I'd yawn under starry skies.

With every dream, I'd tumble and spin,
In a whimsical, gentle waltz.
I woke up and couldn't help but grin,
Thankful for such funny vaults.

Dance of the Night Breeze

The breeze whispers secrets near,
As I trip over my own shoe.
A moth flutters, with no fear,
Daring me to join its crew.

We spun and twirled like wild leaves,
With giggles that filled the night air.
Caught up in dreams, almost believes,
That this dance was beyond compare.

A squirrel peeked, quite astounded,
As I waved to a passing star.
To my surprise, joy bounded,
From my dance, not too bizarre.

I bowed to the end of the show,
And the night applauded my fun.
With a giggle, I pushed through the glow,
The breeze said, "That's how it's done!"

Shadows of a Quiet Twilight

In the dusk, shadows start to play,
I stumble, I slip, I sway.
Cats in hats laugh away,
While I try to save the day.

A firefly flickers, what a sight,
It twirls around my wrinkled grin.
With its tiny, sparkling light,
We're dancing away our chagrin.

The moon peeks from behind a cloud,
Encouraging my wobbly dance.
I twirl, I leap, feeling proud,
As a frog joins in my prance.

With a leap and a graceful bow,
I proclaim this a silly spree.
In this twilight, I take a vow,
To never let the dance flee.

Reflection of Stars

I tripped on a rock, my shoe took flight,
The stars above giggled, oh what a sight!
They whispered sweet jokes, in a twinkling glee,
As I danced with the daffodils, wild and free.

My shadow made faces, oh what a tease,
It spun like a whirligig, floated like leaves.
A comet zoomed past with a wink and a grin,
Said, "Mind your step, don't let the fun end!"

A moonbeam caught me, tried to take me along,
But I laughed it off, claiming I'm strong.
The cosmos rejoiced, with laughter and cheer,
"Let's have a party, all your friends are here!"

The night turned to mischief, oh what a thrill,
Stars danced in circles, it gave me a chill.
In this galaxy of giggles, I zigged and I zagged,
All for a sparkly moment that gladness dragged!

Enchanted Evening Walk

The crickets were crooning, a catchy tune,
As I strolled through the park, under the moon.
A squirrel with a hat offered me a snack,
Said, "Join my soirée, there's no turning back!"

The flowers were gossiping, petals all aflutter,
Spicy secrets to share, all in a mutter.
I chuckled aloud, they all turned to stare,
"Who knew blooms could gawk with such flair?"

A bench said, "Come sit, you've got tales to spin,"
I shared my adventures, what a goofy win!
The stars leaned in closer, amazed and perplexed,
As I spun wild stories, they gasped, "What's next?"

From shadows came shadows, each one with a grin,
They joined the silliness, made my head spin.
Underneath giggling skies, in the night's whirl,
I'll take this odd journey, with a twirl and a twirl!

Silvery Dreams

In a dream I went flying, on a marshmallow cloud,
With unicorns dancing, they were so proud.
A wizard with glasses brewed soda pop,
Said, "Hop on my broomstick, we'll never stop!"

We zipped through the starlight, a carnival scene,
Cotton candy planets and a big jelly bean.
I giggled with fairies, each one had a twirl,
Spinning around in a sparkly swirl.

The moon threw a party with snacks made of cheese,
"Come join us, my friend, I'll share all my keys!"
I munched on the stardust, as laughter took flight,
Twirling through silver, in the heart of the night.

But then I woke up, with a bright morning glow,
Dreams drifted away, like a soft river flow.
Yet in my heart danced, the magic and fun,
I'll chase those silvery dreams, 'til the day is done!

Pathways of Light

Strolling along streets, with moon lanterns bright,
A parade of shadows showcased their delight.
I followed a star that was winking at me,
"Come join the adventure, you'll laugh with glee!"

The pavement was glowing, neon green and blue,
With each step I took, it giggled and flew.
A dog with a top hat asked me for a dance,
Said, "Life's a grand ball, come take a chance!"

A band of wild butterflies swirled in a rush,
They painted the air with a colorful hush.
With a wink and a spin, they called me to play,
In this vibrant world, I'd never stray.

As night turned to laughter, under stars twinkling bright,
I realized these pathways, were pure delight.
In the company of giggles, I shouted, "Oh, joy!"
For every funny moment, my heart it did buoy!

Celestial Illuminations

A raccoon with a hat on his head,
Searching for snacks where the starlight led.
He danced with a comet, quite out of beat,
While milky way sprinkles fell down like sweet.

With a wink to the stars and a shimmy so bold,
He bragged to the moon, 'I'm the best sight to behold!'
But tripped on a beam, and oh what a sight,
He tumbled and rolled, a most comical flight.

Shooting stars giggled, twinkling with glee,
'Is that really a raccoon or a cat in a tree?'
As laughter erupted across the vast sky,
The raccoon just shrugged—'It's a big pie to fly!'

So here's to the night, where silliness grows,
With creatures and watchmen and mishaps, who knows?
For laughter ignites when all shadows unite,
In the glow of the heavens, oh what a delight!

Shadows and Dreams

There's a squirrel in shades, plotting up schemes,
With dreams of the moon, oh, what fun, it seems!
He clings to a branch with a snack in each paw,
While giggling with shadows that whisper and caw.

A shadowy dog, with a grin ear to ear,
Joined in the fun, pulling pranks without fear.
They painted the night with their laughter and light,
And danced 'til they stumbled, oh what a sight!

The stars held their breath, what a silly display,
As the duo concocted wild plans for the day.
'Let's build a moon castle with jellybeans bright,'
The squirrel proclaimed, 'We'll own the whole night!'

So spin, twist, and tumble, let joy be your guide,
In the realm of the shadows, let fun be your ride.
For laughter's the magic that brings us all near,
While dreams take us higher, shedding all fear!

Night's Embrace

In the hush of the night, a turtle did slide,
With a top hat and cane, he was full of pride.
He'd twirl on his shell, to the rhythm of breeze,
While crickets played music, quite eager to please.

A fox in a scarf joined the turtle's parade,
With a jig and a wig, oh, what a charade!
Together they spun, round the light of the stars,
While giggles and chuckles flew far like guitars.

The moon peeked down, with a wink and a grin,
'What's this festive party? Oh let's all jump in!'
So stars twinkled brightly, in harmony bold,
As animals frolicked, their stories retold.

So gather your mates, let the music take flight,
In the embrace of the night, everything feels right.
With laughter and fun, let your spirit unwind,
As dreams dance around in the joy that you find!

Celestial Footprints

A penguin on stilts, with a top coat so fine,
Strolled boldly along, calling 'This star is mine!'
He slipped on a cloud, fell right on his back,
Spinning like pizza with laughter to track.

A walrus nearby chuckled, with ease in his sway,
'Get off my star, buddy! You'll roll it away!'
With flippers a-waving and giggles in tow,
They formed a mad race, let the chaos flow.

The aliens above, in their glimmering ships,
Waved funny flags and made comical quips.
'Are those footprints of joy, or just slippery slides?
In the cosmic chaos, where silliness hides?'

So revel in stardust, and dance through the night,
With penguins and walrus, it's pure delight!
For joy knows no bounds in this starry expanse,
As we leap through the cosmos, let laughter enhance!

Celestial Stroll

Under the stars I glide so free,
Tripping on dreams and a cup of tea.
The cosmos laughs, it's quite the sight,
As I dance with shadows in the soft moonlight.

Asteroids wobble, they join the spree,
Even the comets seem to agree.
"Who needs a partner, just take a chance!"
The universe whispers, "Let's do the Galactic Dance!"

Space turtles grin, looking quite keen,
In this celestial party, I'm a dancing machine.
Gravity's skipping, I'm up in the air,
With my feet on the stars, without a care.

Wishing on a meteor, oh what a treat,
While aliens chuckle, tapping their feet.
If we all just funked through the cosmic tide,
We'd find a groove where the stars collide!

Nightfall Reflections

Pigeons pose as they settle down,
They judge my moves with a sideway frown.
"Who is that fool beneath the glow?"
I wink at the moon, putting on a show.

With twinkling stars as my guiding crew,
I moonwalk backward while the night is new.
"Is that a dance or just a fall?"
Laughter echoes, I hear it all.

Chasing shadows, the fun never ends,
As night unfolds, I'm making friends.
The crickets chirp, they hum along,
In this quirky tune, I find my song.

Reflections swirl like leaves in flight,
As I groove my way till the morning light.
In this garden of whimsy where darkness plays,
I'll be the star for a thousand days!

Whispers of the Night Sky

The bats are giggling, swooping low,
While I waltz with the stars, putting on a show.
"Is he an astronaut or just a clown?"
I twirl in my pajamas, not a care to be found.

Moonbeams tickle my toes so bright,
I stumble on shadows, what a sight!
The owls hoot, rolling their eyes,
As I juggle thoughts 'neath the velvet skies.

Twirling through constellations, what a fun ride,
With every laugh, I feel more alive.
Starlight beams and laughter ignite,
In this wacky dance under the night!

"Just follow my lead!" I playfully shout,
While the universe echoes my silly tout.
Together we whirl through this comic ballet,
As falling stars wish for a brighter day!

Radiant Echoes

Galaxies giggle in colors so bright,
As I float along in the heart of the night.
Jumps and flips, all with flair,
Even the planets can't help but stare.

Slipping on stardust, I find my groove,
With cosmic rhythms inspiring my move.
Shooting stars join in with a cheer,
It's a wild ride, the night's sincere.

"Just a moment," says Saturn with rings,
"Let me spin here, let's see what it brings!"
While Earth chuckles at my silly sway,
In this bright spectacle, I just might stay.

With laughter resounding through time and space,
I embrace every twirl with a silly face.
The echoes of joy fill the cosmic sea,
In my radiant dance, I'm finally free!

Serenity Under Stars

The night sky giggles, stars are bright,
A cat with moonlight hones her sight.
She pounces softly, then slips away,
In a waltz with shadows, she loves to play.

A comet races, with a whoosh and a cheer,
While astronauts chuckle, sipping their beer.
The cosmos winks, all is a jest,
Even the milky way knows how to fest!

Uncle Saturn shouts, 'Come join the fun!'
While Mercury dances, swift as a gun.
The stars are laughing, in cosmic ballet,
Feeling jolly on this starry display.

In the arms of the night, all worries cease,
As the universe chuckles, granting us peace.
So let's float among them, and enjoy the sight,
For this is a playground, dressed in starlight!

Starlit Musings

A shooting star fell, what a sight!
Expecting a wish? Nah, it's just flight.
Over the grassy hills it whizzed,
Laughing at wishes that simply fizzed.

The moon twirls round, thinking it's grand,
While the sun yells, 'Hey, that wasn't planned!'
Galaxies chuckle, hugging tight,
'Who knew space could be so light?'

Constellations whisper, sharing their lore,
Pisces just joked, 'I've been here before.'
Little stars giggle, in a sparkly line,
Saying, 'Time's just a relative design!'

In this cosmic comedy, joy is the key,
Dance with the starlight, come, follow me!
Sip on the laughter, let worries part,
For the universe thrives with a jubilant heart!

Wandering the Moonlit Path

Under the glow of a big cheese wheel,
A rabbit hops past, announcing a meal.
Was that a shadow or a giggling sprite?
Only the moon knows on this funny night.

Footsteps are tricky in silver-soaked light,
Tripping on stardust feels just right.
The crickets croon beneath the gleam,
As fireflies join in, weaving a dream.

A raccoon in sunglasses, oh what a sight!
Singing a tune, under moonshine bright.
'What's your wish?' he asks with a grin,
'A dance with the stars? Well, let's begin!'

Wandering softly, my laughter ignites,
As shadows perform in their peculiar tights.
With every step, giggles take flight,
On the moonlit path, feelings are light!

Celestial Dreams

The cosmos is a stage, glittering with flair,
A cosmic drama with antics to spare.
Stars twinkle boldly, with jokes in their beams,
Laughing at life, in our celestial dreams.

Planets take turns in a merry-go-round,
Mars spins with joy, making everyone astound.
Saturn throws rings, a playful parade,
While Neptune's dance moves never seem to fade.

A shooting star whispers a pun in flight,
'Why don't meteors ever get in a fight?'
With casual grins, they bounce off the seams,
In this grand play where reality beams.

So join the laughter, let your heart sway,
In the universe's humor, find your own play.
Celestial dreams hold freedom so bright,
Unraveling joy on this star-laden night!

Walks in Enchanted Nightscapes

Under the glow of a silver orb,
I tripped on my own two feet,
Chased shadows, they danced with glee,
While crickets sang a funny beat.

I saw a cat in a bowtie,
Dancing like it owned the show,
I laughed so hard, I nearly cried,
As the moon winked, with a soft glow.

A raccoon joined in on the fun,
With a hat that had a flair,
He stole my sandwich on the run,
Leaving behind a sticky glare.

The night was filled with giggles bright,
As stars joined in a silly dance,
In the glow of the whimsical light,
We all took part in this strange chance.

Starry Reveries

Gazing up, I saw a star,
Winking at a passing cloud,
I wondered if it lived too far,
And if it's ever feeling loud.

A comet zoomed with a flashy tail,
I shouted, "Hey, don't crash!"
It laughed and left a sparkling trail,
Making my silly dream a smash.

I tried to catch a shooting star,
With a net made of old cheese lace,
But it zipped right past, quite bizarre,
Leaving behind a twinkling trace.

The night was full of cosmic pranks,
As planets played hide and seek,
With giggles echoed in their ranks,
And starlight made us all feel chic.

Illuminated Reflections

In the pond, I saw my face,
Reflected by the moon's soft light,
I waved and made a funny face,
It answered back, what a delight!

A frog croaked a comical tune,
As fireflies twirled in the air,
I joined the dance beneath the moon,
With laughter bouncing everywhere.

I dropped my shoe into the lake,
And watched the ripples laugh and sway,
The fish made jokes that made me quake,
Under the silver beams of play.

With each step, the shadows pranced,
As I spun in a goofy whirl,
In this joy, I lost my chance,
But found a new silly pearl.

Celestial Conversations

I had a chat with Mr. Sun,
He laughed, said, "You're quite a clown!"
"Why do you think you're on the run?"
As I slipped and fell right down.

The stars just giggled in the night,
Said they'd tell tales of my trip,
I blushed beneath their sparkling light,
As I tried not to let it rip.

The moon said, "You're a funny thing!"
While I danced like no one would see,
I twirled and tripped, without a sting,
In this cosmic comedy spree.

So here I am, with my celestial crew,
Joking 'neath the midnight hue,
With every giggle that we strew,
We add more laughter to the blue.

Cosmic Wanderings

Stars spill secrets, oh so bright,
While aliens dance in the pale moonlight.
A comet sneezes, what a sight!
In this space circus, everything's alright.

Asteroids make the best of friends,
Tossing popcorn while the universe bends.
Jupiter juggles, Saturn descends,
In this cosmic chaos, joy never ends.

Midnight Meditations

I sat with craters, deep in thought,
What do they say about the battles fought?
The quiet lunar winds, they caught,
Whispers of cheese—oh, what a spot!

Philosophers in orbit, all topsy-turvy,
Discussing gravity while feeling groggy.
They all agree, it's rather foggy,
But laughter rains like confetti, how snappy!

Dreamer's Tango

Two stars waltz under a blanket of dark,
With twinkling toes, they make their mark.
Planets giggle, a playful lark,
In this galactic dance, they leave a spark.

They trip on stardust with charming flair,
As comets swirl, they breathe the air.
A jovial spin, without a care,
In this cosmic ball, all hearts laid bare.

Luminous Footsteps

With glowing shoes, I bounce around,
Leaving sparkles on the ground.
The Milky Way hums a joyous sound,
As I stomp in rhythm—what a playground!

Shooting stars join the silly race,
Flipping and flapping in outer space.
This cosmic hop, a funny chase,
In every leap, the universe I embrace.

Voyage Under the Moon

Bouncing high on silvery beams,
I stumbled over cosmic seams.
The stars laughed as I slipped and twirled,
While chasing dreams in a zero-gravity world.

My socks are floating, what a sight!
I could dance with aliens all night.
But wait, there goes my sandwich too,
Guess it's a cosmic picnic for me and you!

As I twirl through space, what do I see?
A critter waving from a space debris!
It juggled planets, oh what a show,
I joined the fun, enjoying the flow.

So here I am on this wacky ride,
With laughter echoing far and wide.
Who knew that space was such a blast?
I'll bounce forever, holding on fast!

Footprints on Cosmic Sands

I left my mark on the Milky Way,
Tried to write my name, but it slipped away.
Footprints in stardust, faded and bright,
A space-age tango, what a sight!

Dancing with comets, spinning with flair,
Legs are tangled; do I really care?
My shadow's a cartoon, adding some fun,
As I chase after light, oh, what a run!

Sand from Saturn made a soft bed,
I woke up with meteors dancing in my head.
They told me stories of cosmic fame,
Each tale a giggle, each laugh a claim.

So, if you're lost in the starry spree,
Just follow my footprints, come dance with me.
Together we'll waltz on celestial shores,
In a silly search for the moon's hidden doors!

Serenade of Astral Light

With a ukulele and stars overhead,
I strummed a tune right out of my head.
Jupiter tossed in some funky bass,
While Saturn spun 'round with a grin on its face.

The Milky Way joined in, quite a band,
Singing harmonies, oh so grand.
Asteroids clapped, what a show!
Grooving along, wouldn't you know?

But then I tripped on a starlit note,
Flipped in the air like a silly old goat.
My cosmic crowd burst into glee,
As I landed softly on E.T.'s knee!

So let's keep jamming till dawn does break,
With cosmic rhythms, we'll shake and quake.
In this twisty waltz through the infinite night,
We'll fill the void with our silly delight!

Lullabies from the Ether

Floating softly, with stars all around,
I crooned sleepy tunes without making a sound.
The cosmos swayed to my gentle hum,
Rocking the planets, a lullaby strum.

Luna smirked as I sang to the dark,
While Orions danced, leaving their mark.
I watched as meteors winked at my rhyme,
In this sleepy ballet, we drift through time.

As comets zoomed by on their midnight flight,
I whispered sweet dreams, oh what a sight!
The galaxy chuckled, twinkling with glee,
An interstellar nap, just you and me.

So snuggle up close in this ether's embrace,
With lullabies flowing from this cozy space.
Together we'll dream until morning is near,
With laughter and starlight, no worries, no fear!

Ribbons of Dark

In the blanket of night, I twirl and spin,
Tripping on shadows, let the giggles begin.
The moon is a spotlight on my dance floor,
Yet my two left feet have me begging for more.

Stars are my partners in this wacky waltz,
With each little stumble, I can't help but fault.
The comets cheer on as I tumble astound,
While crickets laugh loudly, oh what a sound!

I leap over puddles that sparkle like gold,
With dreams in my pockets, my mischief is bold.
An owl hoots a rhythm, I shimmy and shake,
In the dark, I find joy, not a single mistake!

With a twinkle and twist, I declare this parade,
Silly midnight antics—come join in, I said!
Laughter and moonlight, a combo divine,
In ribbons of dark, we all brightly shine.

Journey Through the Night

Under starry skies, I ride a wild wave,
Bouncing on moonbeams feels just like a rave.
Each step is a dance, each giggle's a tune,
As I prance with the shadows beneath the full moon.

I meet a raccoon with a hat and a grin,
He nods to the beat as we both start to spin.
A squirrel joins in, wearing socks that don't match,
Together we stomp, what a wacky old batch!

The night is a carnival, so colorful, bright,
With whispers of wind that pull me in tight.
A cat on a fence gives a wink and a sigh,
And I dare him to join me—oh me, oh my!

On this journey of fun, every bump is a laugh,
As we dance through the dark, we craft our own path.
So, let's take a ride on this whimsical flight,
And cherish the joy of a journey through night!

Shadows of the Stars

Beneath the sky, I twirl and glide,
My feet are light, my heart full wide.
A deer looks on, with a puzzled gaze,
Did they really just see me sway in a daze?

The moon is laughing, shining bright,
Calling for dancers in the middle of night.
I trip on my shoelace, oh what a scene,
Who knew my shoes brought on such a routine?

The stars are winking, they join the game,
I spin and leap, they chant my name.
But just as I jump, I lose my shoe,
Now it's a chase, oh what can I do?

With shadows as friends, we play and spin,
Each foxtrot and tango, I laugh with a grin.
The night's a stage, both bright and strange,
And I'm the star in this odd little range.

Ethereal Walks

Underneath the stars, I prance about,
My friends are giggling, there's no doubt.
We spin like planets, round and round,
Hoping to trip on laughter's sound.

A comet zips by, aren't we all brave?
Dodging space rocks, oh the things we crave!
My socks don't match, oh well, who cares?
In this cosmic dance, fashion's for bears!

With whispers of starlight, we glide and bounce,
The aliens peek in, surely they pounce.
They join our jig with a curious swoosh,
The universe chuckles, what a big whoosh!

Gravity's joking, as I hit the ground,
It flips me like pancakes, oh, what a sound!
But laughter's a pillow, soft and so fine,
We roll like tumbleweeds, all intertwined.

Starlight Surreal

With a hat that's floppy and shoes like two clowns,
I glide on the beams while everyone frowns.
"Look at that dancer!" they giggle and clap,
But little do they know, it's all just a trap.

The stars tumble down, laughing so loud,
As I execute moves that draw quite a crowd.
A misstep turns into an unexpected slide,
My dance turns to tumble, oh what a ride!

I topple like dominoes—what a display,
My feet like spaghetti, no roads to okay.
The moon shakes its head, oh what a sight,
As I twist and I twirl, lost in the night.

But spirits aren't dampened, we just swap our shoes,
Now the stars are winking, they've joined in the blues.
We dance in a circle, through giggles and twirls,
Finding joy in the chaos that life unfurls.

Drift of the Dusk

I strolled through the dusk with a hop and a skip,
Found a puddle—oh what a dip!
Pranced right through, created a splash,
The reflection of me? A starlit clash!

A bat swooped down, but missed the cue,
Thought I was a berry, a wild rendezvous.
"Fly up high!" I shouted with laughter so spry,
While he zoomed away with a terrified cry.

The moon peeks through clouds with a knowing smirk,
As I whirl my arms, oh what a quirk!
Neighbors smile from windows, enjoying the spree,
"Is that our friend? What a sight to see!"

So with the stars above and laughter around,
In this crazy dance, joy is the sound.
I twirl with delight under celestial praise,
Finding humor in night's whimsical ways.

Twilight's Soft Serenade

Under the glow of a disco ball,
The bats throw a dance, oh what a ball!
Squirrels in tuxedos, they hop and sway,
As shadows play games till the break of day.

Stars wink down from their velvet throne,
While crickets hum tunes in a mischievous tone.
A fox with a top hat struts by with flair,
In this twilight party, there's fun everywhere.

The moon's got a grin, he's the life of the scene,
Whispering secrets to frogs so keen.
They croak in delight, a bass line so deep,
While stars flip pancakes that sizzle and beep.

As dawn starts to creep, they start to retreat,
This night of good jokes was ever so sweet.
But promise, dear friends, we'll meet here again,
For comedy reigns when the sun's down, amen!

Phases of a Starlit Journey

Oh, the plot thickens under a glowing sphere,
Where raccoons debate what snacks to revere.
One swears by cookies while others go for fries,
Each choice is a winner in those twinkling eyes.

A snail in a shell wears a jacket so neat,
He's the slowest of runners, but thinks he's quite fleet.
He shouts, "Catch up, everyone! Life's a race!"
While fireflies giggle, lighting up the space.

The owl gives a hoot; it's a night for a thrill,
Suggesting a game of hide and seek still.
With laughter and squeals, the night takes a turn,
As stars shift and twirl, for their moments we yearn.

But just as it peaks, the sun starts to peek,
The creatures retreat from their playful mystique.
"Same time tomorrow!" they cheer and agree,
In this starlit journey, we feel young and free!

The Secret Life of Night Walks

Tiptoe through shadows, a gleam in the night,
Where noses poke pie pans, what a funny sight!
The neighbor's old cat gives a scandalous stare,
"What are you up to? You've lost all your hair!"

Dancing past bushes, this breeze is a tease,
With whispers of laughter on rustling leaves.
A hedgehog wearing glasses reads poetry loud,
His audience chuckles, feeling quite proud.

"Did you hear the one 'bout the frog on a log?"
"Who croaked out a joke 'bout a hot dog's fog?"
Oh, nightly escapades, bubbling with cheer,
A sing-song of giggles as dawn draws near.

But soon it'll end, with a wink to the sky,
"See you next week!" calls a wave and a sigh.
Secret lives linger in shadows and gleam,
Turning night walks timeless, fulfilling a dream.

Astral Dances of Thought

Steps that are light, in the cool of the night,
I ponder a dance with a firefly's light.
Does he lead or follow in this twinkling game?
We two share thought bubbles, igniting the flame.

The stars clap their hands, or is that just me?
Perhaps they're all laughing at how I can't see.
A comet whizzes by with a cheeky grin,
"Wanna race?" it calls, "Let the fun times begin!"

In the midst of my thoughts, a raccoon sneaks by,
Stealing my sandwich—and oh, my oh my!
With crumbs on his face, he dashes away,
While giggling at shadows that choose to play.

As dawn waves a hand, bidding us goodbye,
I'm left with a chuckle and dreams in the sky.
For each little moment a story can birth,
In astral dances, we find what it's worth.

Cosmic Footfalls

On cosmic ground, I skip and hop,
My footfalls make the star-dust pop.
With each leap, I laugh and twirl,
In zero-g, the galaxy's my whirl.

I met a comet, gave it a spin,
It winked at me, said, "Let's begin!"
We danced around a distant star,
While aliens laughed, we took it far.

I tripped on Saturn's rings with glee,
The space cat chuckled, 'You're quite free!'
I flipped and flopped like I was daft,
Yet in this dance, found my own craft.

The moonbeams chuckled, bright and clear,
As I tried to moonwalk, full of cheer.
But gravity played its cheeky game,
And down I fell with pride, not shame.

Ramblings of a Lunar Traveler

Upon the moon, I take a stroll,
In my silly suit, I feel quite whole.
Crater hop, then slide with flair,
Lunar dust flies high in air.

I shout to Earth, 'Can you see me?
I'm bouncing high like a jubilee!'
A space mouse scurries by my side,
Together, we bounce with cosmic pride.

I tried to cook a cheese fondue,
But the cheese just floated, who knew?
The stars keep giggling at my plight,
As I feast on snacks in the soft moonlight.

With space dust in my hair, I grin,
The universe laughs; let the fun begin!
In this vast playground, carefree and bold,
I'll dance with the stardust till I'm old.

The Night's Gentle Embrace

Under starlit skies, I prance and play,
As the night whispers secrets of yesterday.
A gentle breeze carries my song,
While the moon insists, 'You can't go wrong!'

I sneak a peek at a shooting star,
Waving hello, from near and far.
It veers and zigzags, oh what a sight,
Chasing my laughter through the night.

Invisible friends join in the game,
With cosmic giggles, they're never the same.
We build our castles in clouds of cheese,
And dance on stardust with cosmic ease.

The night wraps me in an airy hug,
While I wiggle and squirm, like a happy bug.
In this funny chaos, I find my place,
In the universe's heart, I spin and race.

Under the Gaze of Celestial Orbs

Beneath the gaze of twinkling lights,
I juggle planets on whimsical nights.
Each one slips and dances away,
As I crack jokes that stars replay.

I chased a meteor with a leap,
It laughed and said, 'You're in too deep!'
I tripped in orbit, swirling with glee,
The galaxies joined—in perfect spree.

A cosmic cat lay on a star,
Purring tunes that could travel far.
It said, 'Dear traveler, join my game,
We'll dance through space and never be tame!'

With each twist and spin, I hear the cheers,
The universe winks, dissolving fears.
In this frolicsome journey, I find my place,
Under the orbs, I'll always embrace.

Whispers Beneath the Stars

Underneath the twinkling lights,
A cat serenades its newfound heights,
As squirrels dance on silver beams,
   In a night full of silly dreams.

The frogs croak out a midnight tune,
While bats join in, a comical swoon,
The owl winks and tells a joke,
Leaving the moon to simply choke.

A pair of fireflies flash and tease,
Dancing with grace like quirky fees,
And as I laugh, the stars reply,
With giggles that fill the vast sky.

Embracing all the nonsense bright,
We frolic under the night's delight,
In this cosmic circus of surprise,
Where humor reigns and laughter flies.

Lullabies of the Night

The crickets play their soothing song,
While shadows skip and prance along,
A baby raccoon steals my snack,
Making midnight feel like a hack.

Oh, the moon's a cheeky fellow,
Casting beams both bright and yellow,
He chuckles as he lights the way,
For sleepyheads who laugh and play.

A turtle jogs, a hilarious feat,
While two snails race, slow and sweet,
Each lullaby a giggle spun,
Under the stars, we find our fun.

The night is vast, with jokes untold,
In shimmering glimmers, bold and gold,
So close your eyes and hear the cheer,
As nighttime whispers tickle the ear.

The Path of the Celestial

Stumbling through the cosmic swirl,
I trip on stardust, watch it twirl,
A comet zips, a playful blaze,
While I pretend to lose my gaze.

Planets giggle as I pass by,
With their rings swirling, oh so sly,
And then a meteor gives a wink,
Making my stargazing think.

Asteroids toss an interstellar ball,
I chase it down, but I trip and fall,
Laughter echoes in the night sky,
As laughter spreads, oh my oh my!

In this cosmic trail, a silly feat,
Finding humor makes my night complete,
With aliens chuckling, it's quite a show,
On this path where giggles flow.

Nightfall Navigation

I'm lost beneath the glowing light,
Map made of clouds, what a funny sight,
The North Star waves, "Come this way,"
   While I fumble, it leads me astray.

   With constellations grinning wide,
They nudge each other, they can't hide,
   A rabbit hops, a bear's a fluff,
   In cosmic paths, I've had enough!

The Milky Way spills cheese with flair,
   I bring crackers, what a rare affair,
So cheese-filled nights become a feast,
   With a tape measure, I am least.

Navigating through the nighttime cheer,
   With giggles near and laughter clear,
   Each turn I take, a chuckle's found,
In this joyful journey, night's profound.

The Dance of the Night

The stars are wearing their finest tux,
While I trip on my feet like a clumsy fox.
The moon gives a wink, a cheeky little grin,
As I sway and I spin, feeling tipsy within.

The shadows join in with a jig and a hop,
While nocturnal critters just can't seem to stop.
I'm twirling through dreams, oh, what a delight,
In this dance of the night, everything feels right.

But wait, what's that? Is it a cat on the floor?
Nope, it's my own shoelace, wanting to soar.
The creatures all laugh; they're having a ball,
While I'm bound to the ground, unable to crawl.

Yet with every misstep, I laugh even more,
The night is alive, and I'm ready to soar!
So let's raise a glass to the wobbly dance,
Where laughter and joy lead the night in a trance.

Serenade of the Universe

In the cosmic kitchen, the stars cook up dreams,
While I spill my soda and burst at the seams.
The planets all giggle, a galactic delight,
As I try to impress them with moves all too bright.

My socks have a rhythm, they slide 'cross the floor,
And suddenly I find I've opened a door.
The galaxies join in, a celestial spree,
As I pirouette wildly, oh, what a sight to see!

Asteroids chuckle while comets take flight,
Joining the rave in the shimmering night.
I spin with a grin, oh, what a weird show,
In this serenade, I'm the star of the low!

Yet somehow I churn like a disco ball wreck,
As the universe beams, giving life a good heck.
So here's to the dance, both silly and grand,
In the grand serenade, I'll always take a stand.

Echoes of Twilight

As twilight creeps in, the crickets applaud,
While I trip on an acorn, how very unflawed.
The fireflies flicker like tiny disco lights,
As I bust out the moves under starry delights.

With a wink from the sky, the silliness grows,
As I twirl with the moonbeams, my footwork's a show.
The trees sway along, giving branches a wave,
While I attempt my best not to fall in the grave.

But what is this chaos? A slip, then I fly,
The echoing laughter, oh my, oh my!
The owls hoot a tune, a chorus of glee,
As I roll on the grass, feeling ever so free.

In this echo of twilight, filled with silly grace,
I dance like no one, lost in this embrace.
So let lightheartedness guide you through the night,
Join me in this frenzy; it just feels so right!

Illuminated Wanderings

Wandering under the glow of the night,
My shoes look to tango; my heart feels so light.
The stars greet my feet with a shimmy and shake,
As I pop and I lock for the universe's sake.

With each little twirl, the sky starts to swirl,
And my dance moves make even stardust all whirl.
The comets give chase, in a giggle-filled race,
While I trip on my laces, oh what a disgrace!

But laughter ignites, and the cosmos can't stop,
As I whirl and I twirl near the moonlit crop.
The galaxies cheer, throwing hands in the air,
While I'm grounded and laughing, lost without care.

So here's to the nights filled with sparkles and gleam,
Where I dance like a fool, living out every dream.
In these illuminated wanderings, wild and grand,
Life's better with laughter, come take my hand!

Night's Quiet Symphony

The stars are a chatter, oh what a sight,
A squirrel strums a tree branch, lost in delight.
The crickets join in, with their tiny guitars,
While fireflies dance like ambitious little stars.

The moon winks down with a sly little grin,
As raccoons start planning their nighttime din.
A cat spreads its paws on the rooftop's peak,
Declaring itself king with an elegant squeak.

Astrological Whispers

The constellations plot, with a flick and a flare,
Venus just told Mars that it's getting quite rare.
Jupiter's hooting, making grand cosmic plans,
While comets gossip, serving space gossip fans.

A turtle in stardust wears a cap quite low,
Claiming it's faster than any shooting show.
And Saturn's rings giggle, oh what a parade,
They twirl and they spin, in a galaxy charade.

Twilight Tranquility

The frogs hold a concert, with croaks in the air,
Robins are laughing—what a riot down there!
As shadows grow longer, a deer pulls a prank,
While watching the horizon, it starts to prank.

The owls are hooting, wearing spectacles bright,
Debating their wisdom well into the night.
A turtle in twilight takes the slowest of strolls,
As fireflies glow, Googling cosmic roles.

Veil of the Nightfall

The night begins weaving its silky black thread,
As squirrels set out to count all the stars overhead.
The laughter of shadows fills up the fresh air,
While wishes on dandelions float everywhere.

With a twinkle and jig, the moon starts to tease,
As owls in top hats attempt to out-sneeze.
A fox with a flair puts on its best show,
Claiming the night like a flamboyant pro.

www.ingramcontent.com/pod-product-compliance
Lightning Source LLC
Chambersburg PA
CBHW051650160426
43209CB00004B/863